Cocoa's Fun Recipes

Kid's Cookbook
Healthy & Easy-to-Make Recipes

by Yokima Arias

Cocoa's Fun Recipes: Kid's Cookbook Healthy & Easy-to-Make Recipes

This publication and its materials are not intended for use as a source of legal, financial, professional, physical health, or medical advice. As with any business or experience, your results may vary, and will be based on your individual capacity, expertise, and effort. There are no guarantees concerning the results and success you may experience.

Stock Photos are from Canva

Printed in the United States of America

ISBN: 978-0-578-30492-2

Table of Contents

Smoothies

BY

Cocoa

AND FRIENDS

Green Veggie Smoothie

Green Veggie Smoothie

Ingredients

3/4 cup Almond milk

1 medium banana

1 green apple

1/2 cup frozen mango chunks

1 tbsp. Rolled oats

1 cup Baby spinach

2 tbsp. nut butter

1/2 tsp vanilla

Instructions

Put all ingredients into
a blender. Blend until smooth
Serve

The Refreshing Fruit Juice

100% ORGANIC

The Refreshing Fruit Juice

DIRECTIONS

- Cut watermelons into small cubes.
- Put watermelon cubes and ice in a blender and blend.
- The refreshing drink is ready.

BERRY

Smoothie

only two ingredients

BERRY
Smoothie

INGREDIENTS:
- Frozen Berries
- Almond Milk
- Honey(optional)

DIRECTIONS:
- Place berries, almond milk, and honey in a blender.
- Blend and Enjoy

Strawberry
Yogurt

Milk

Strawberry
Yogurt

Ingredients

16 oz. Greek yogurt

2 cups rolled oats

16 oz. Frozen strawberries

Instructions

Put yogurt, oats, and strawberries in a blender.

Blend until fully combined.

Garnish with fresh strawberries and serve.

Strawberry & Banana Smoothie

Strawberry & Banana Smoothie

Ingredients

- 1 banana
- 5-7 strawberries
- 2 tbsps rolled oatmeal
- 1 scoop vanilla protein powder
- 1 tablespoon smooth peanut butter
- 1 cup unsweetened almond milk

Instructions

1. Place everything into a blender.
2. Blend on high, stopping to scrape the sides as needed, until smooth.
3. Serve immediately!

Snacks
by
Cocoa
and friends

Fruit Popsicles

13

Fruity Popsicle

Ingredients

Fruit of your choice

Honey

Lemon juice

Method

Put all ingredients into a blender. Blend well.

Pour in moulds

Freeze overnight.

3 INGREDIENTS FRUITY TREAT

3 Ingredients
Fruity Treat

INGREDIENTS

Frozen Fruit

Greek yogurt

honey

Method

- Place all ingredients in a food processor.
- Blend it well.
- Freeze
- Serve

16

Chocolate Dipped

Banana

Chocolate dipped

Banana

Ingredients

8-ounce semi-sweet choco...

popsicle sticks

2 bananas cut into thirds

1/3 cup coarsely chopped peanuts

Instructions

Melt chocolate while continuously
stirring. Line a baking tray with
waxed paper.

Insert a popsicle stick in each banana.
Dip it in chocolate.

Sprinkle with peanuts. Refrigerate
before serving.

18

Blueberry Muffin

19

Blueberry Muffin

Ingredients

1 ¾ cups whole wheat flour

1 tsp baking powder

½ tsp baking soda

½ tsp sea salt

¼ tsp ground cinnamon

⅓ cup melted coconut oil

½ cup honey

2 eggs

1 cup plain greek yogurt

2 tsp vanilla extract

1 cup (6 ounces) blueberries

1 tablespoon icing sugar

Instructions

Preheat the oven to 400 degrees Fahrenheit.

In a large mixing bowl, combine flour, baking powder, baking soda, salt, and cinnamon.

In a medium mixing bowl, combine the oil and honey and beat together. Add the eggs, yogurt, and vanilla. Mix well.

Pour the wet ingredients into the dry and mix with a big spoon, just until combined.

Tossing the blueberries with the remaining 1 teaspoon flour (this helps prevent the blueberries from sinking to the bottom). Gently fold the blueberries into the batter.

Divide the batter evenly between the 12 muffin cups. Bake the muffins for 16 to 19 minutes, or until a toothpick inserted into a muffin comes out clean.

Protein

Balls

Protein Balls

INGREDIENTS

- 3 cups Medjool dates pitted
- 1 1/2 cups almonds
- 1/2 cup water
- 2 tbsp cacao powder
- 120 g whey protein powder
- 1/4 cup dark chocolate chips
- 1/2 cup coconut flakes

METHOD

1 Add ingredients to a food processor
2 Make balls in your hand
3 Place in fridge. Devour!

Fig and Peanut Butter Bliss Balls

Bliss Balls

Ingredients

- 14 dried figs
- 200g raw or roasted peanuts
- 4 tbsp 100% natural peanut butter
- 1 tbsp cacao powder
- 1-2 tbsp water, if needed

Method

1. Line a baking tray with baking paper.
2. Place all of the ingredients into a food processor and process.
3. Using your hands, roll the mixture into snack-sized balls.
4. Pour the crushed peanuts onto a plate or flat surface and roll the balls in the nuts to coat.
5. Place them in a prepared tray and refrigerate for 30 minutes. Devour!

No-Bake
Vegan Brownies

Ingredients

1 cup Rolled oats

1 cup Desiccated coconut

1 cup Almonds

1/3cup Cocoa

1/2 cup Dried cranberries

1/3cup Coconut oil

1/4cup Maple syrup

1tsp Vanilla extract

Instructions

Place Oats, coconut, almond, cocoa, cranberries, coconut oil, maple syrup, vanilla into a food processor.

Blitz until finely chopped. Add 1-2 tbs of water if required.

Pour mixture into prepared 20/20 cm square tray.

Sprinkle with coconut flakes. Freeze for 1-2 hours. Cut into squares and Enjoy!

27

Chocolate Chip Cookies

Ingredients

- 3/4 cup granulated brown sugar
- 3/4 cup packed brown sugar
- 1 cup butter
- 1 tsp. vanilla
- 1 egg
- 2 1/4 cups all-purpose flour
- 1 tsp. baking soda
- 1/2 teaspoon salt
- 1 cup coarsely chopped nuts
- 12 ounces semisweet chocolate chips (2 cups)

Directions

- Heat oven to 375°F.
- Mix sugars, butter, vanilla, and egg in a large bowl. Stir in flour, baking soda, and salt (dough will be stiff). Stir in nuts and chocolate chips.
- Drop dough by rounded tablespoonfuls about 2 inches apart onto an ungreased cookie sheet. Bake 8 to 10 minutes or until light brown
- (centers will be soft). Cool slightly; remove from cookie sheet.
- Cool on wire rack.
- Enjoy.

Fruit Kabobs

Ingredients

1 cup strawberries tops cut off
1 cup cantaloupe cubed
1 cup pineapple cubed
1/2 cup Kiwi peeled and sliced
1/2 cup red grapes
1/2 cup blackberries

Instructions

- Prepare all fruit by washing and cutting or cubing.
- Add fruit onto skewers in rainbow order, piercing through the sharp side. Strawberries, cantaloupe, pineapple, kiwis, red grapes, and blackberries.
- Place on a platter and cover with Saran wrap. Refrigerate until ready to serve.

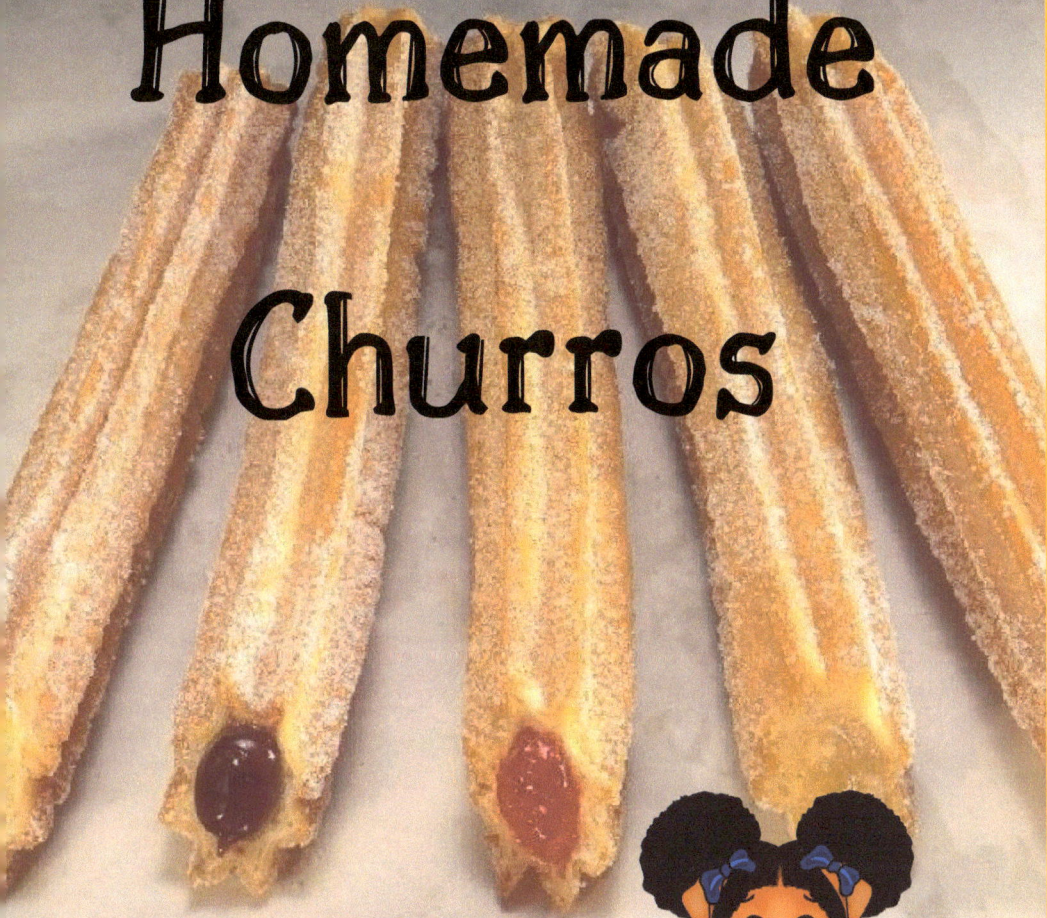

Homemade Churros

Ingredients

- 1 cup water
- 2 1/2 tbsp. sugar 1/2 teaspoon salt 2 tablespoons vegetable oil
- 1 cup flour
- 2 quarts oil for frying
- 1/2 cup white sugar, or to taste
- 1 teaspoon ground cinnamon

Directions

1. In a small saucepan, combine water, 2 1/2 tablespoons sugar, salt, and vegetable oil. Bring to a boil and remove from heat. Stir in flour until the mixture forms a ball.

2. Heat oil for frying in deep-fryer. Pipe strips of dough into hot oil using a pastry bag. Fry until golden; drain on paper towels.

3. Combine 1/2 cup sugar and cinnamon. Roll drained churros in cinnamon and sugar mixture.

Easy

Lunch

Ideas

BY COCOA & FRIENDS

15-minute Homemade Pizza

15-minute Homemade Pizza

Ingredients

- 1 pound pizza dough
- 1/2 to 1 cup tomato sauce
- 2 to 3 cups other toppings: sautéed onions, sautéed mushrooms, pepperoni, cooked sausage, cooked bacon, diced peppers, leftover veggies, or any other favorites
- 1 to 2 cups cheese.

Instructions

- Heat the oven to 550°F or higher Divide the dough in half
- Roll out the dough Top the pizza with your favourite ingredients and cheese
- Bake the pizza for 7 to 10 minutes.
- Slice and serve

Overnight Oats Recipe

Ingredients

- Oats
- Chia Seeds
- Nut Butter (we like Peanut butter)
- Choice of milk
- Fruit
- 100% Maple Syrup

Method

Combine the chia seeds and nut butter.
Add a splash of the milk and
mix the nut butter into the oats.
Then add the rest of the milk
and stir to combine.
Top with your fruit of choice.
Place the lid on the jar and refrigerate
overnight. When you're ready to serve
add a drizzle of maple syrup and
enjoy!

TURKEY WRAP

Ingredients

2 large flour tortillas 10"

4 ounces deli turkey

1 ½ cups lettuce or fresh spinach, shredded

4 large slices of tomato

2 ounces cheddar cheese

¼ cup honey mustard sauce

Instructions

- Warm tortillas slightly in the microwave, about 20 seconds.

- Add 2 tablespoons of honey, mustard to each tortilla.

- Divide remaining ingredients over tortillas. Roll tightly.

- Serve immediately.

Spinach Balls

Spinach Balls

Frozen friendly

Ingredients

2 (10 oz.) packages of spinach

2 small onion

2 cup stuffing with herbs

6 eggs beaten

1/2 cup butter melted

1/2 cup parmesan cheese

2 tsp garlic

Salt and pepper to taste

Method

Drain spinach very well

In a mixing bowl, mix together all ingredients until well combined. Form 1" balls and bake at 350 F for about 20 minutes. Ready to serve.

Healthy
Vegetable
Sandwich

Vegetable Sandwich

Ingredients

- 2 slices bread mayo and mustard 6 leaves romaine lettuce
- freshly ground pepper
- 1 avocado
- Handful of sprouts
- 3 slices tomato
- Slices red onion
- Dried oregano

How to Cook

Spread on mayo and mustard to taste and build your sandwich: 1/2 of the lettuce leaves, carrots, cucumber, salt and pepper, cabbage, avocado, sprouts, tomato, onion, then the remaining lettuce and top slice of bread. Serve with fries.

GREEN PASTA

- 1 pound any pasta
- 6 tablespoons salted butter
- 2-3 cloves garlic, minced or grated
- 1 1/2 teaspoons freshly cracked black pepper
- 1/2 cup parmesan cheese, freshly grated
- 1 cup fresh basil, roughly chopped

INSTRUCTIONS

1. Boil pasta and just before draining, reserve 1 cup of the cooking water. Drain.

2. Melt 4 tablespoons butter in a large skillet over medium heat. Add the garlic and pepper and cook 1-2 minutes, until the garlic is golden and fragrant.

3. Add boiled pasta and basil to it. Add water and let it simmer.

4. Before serving, add freshly grated cheese to it.

Toasted Tuna Sandwich

Toasted Tuna Sandwich

Ingredients

½ Cup Drained Tuna

Flakes

4 Tbsp. Mayonnaise

1 Tsp. Minced Onion

2 Slices Bran Bread

4 Sliced Cucumbers

2 Sliced Tomatoes

Directions

Drain the tuna in a strainer in the sink.
Chop the celery to measure 1/2 cup.
Peel and chop the onion to measure
1/4 cup. Mix the tuna, celery, onion,
mayonnaise, lemon juice, salt and pepper in a
medium bowl. Spread tuna mixture on 4
bread. Top with remaining bread slices.
Enjoy!

48

CURRIED
EGG SALAD SANDWICH RECIPE

INGREDIENTS

SERVE: 4
TOTAL TIME: 20 MIN

8 Large Eggs
1/3 cup Mayonnaise
1 tsp Curry Powder
1 tbs Chopped Fresh Chives
Kosher Salt and Black Pepper
4 Slices Wheat Bread
4 Large Leaves Bibb Lettuce
Potato Chips, for serving

DIRECTIONS

Place the eggs in a saucepan and add enough water to cover. Bring to a boil, cover, remove from heat, and let sit for 12 minutes. Rinse the eggs under cold water, peel, and coarsely chop.

In a medium bowl, combine the mayonnaise and curry powder. Fold in the eggs and chives; season with ½ teaspoon salt and ¼ teaspoon pepper. Dividing evenly, top each slice of bread with lettuce, then the egg salad. Serve with the chips.

Pizza Muffin

Ingredients

1 1/2 cups milk

1 cup grated carrot

1 cup mozzarella cheese

1/4 cup Parmesan cheese

1/4 cup butter or oil

1/4 cup diced pepperoni

2 eggs, lightly beaten

1 cup all-purpose flour

1 cup whole-wheat flour

1 teaspoon baking powder

1/2 teaspoon baking soda

2 teaspoons pizza seasoning

1/2 teaspoon salt

Directions

- Preheat the oven and grease a standard muffin tin tray.
- Add milk, carrot, cheeses, butter, pepperoni (reserving the 2 tablespoons), and egg to a medium bowl. Mix. Stir in the flours, baking powder, baking soda, pizza seasoning, and salt. Put batter in a muffin tin.
- Bake for 18-20 minutes or until a cake tester inserted into the center comes out clean. Muffins are ready. Enjoy!

Mini Turkey Burgers

Ingredients

2 slices white bread

1 pound ground turkey

2 ounces cheddar cheese

1/2 small onion,

coarsely grated

Salt and pepper to taste

1 teaspoon olive oil

12 party-size rolls

Lettuce, sliced tomatoes

Directions

In a food processor, pulse bread, turkey, cheese, and onion.

Season with salt and pepper, and mix gently just until combined. Form twelve 2-inch patties (about 3 tablespoons each).

Heat oil over medium heat. Cook patties until browned and cooked through, about 5 minutes per side. Serve on rolls with lettuce, tomatoes, and sweet potato fries, if desired.

www.ingramcontent.com/pod-product-compliance
Lightning Source LLC
Chambersburg PA
CBHW041950110426

42744CB00026B/7